DRAW ALONG Animals

Pippa Pixley

Author & Illustrator Pippa Pixley
Editor Abi Luscombe
Designer Brandie Tully-Scott
US Editor Jane Perlmutter
Managing Editor Gemma Farr
Managing Art Editor Diane Peyton Jones
Production Editor Becky Fallowfield
Senior Production Controller Ben Radley
Jacket Designer Brandie Tully-Scott

First American Edition, 2025
Published in the United States by DK Publishing,
a division of Penguin Random House LLC
1745 Broadway, 20th Floor, New York, NY 10019

Text and Illustration copyright © Pippa Pixley 2025
Design copyright © 2025 Dorling Kindersley Limited
24 25 26 27 28 10 9 8 7 6 5 4 3 2 1
001–341063–Apr/2025

All rights reserved.
Without limiting the rights under the copyright reserved above, no part of this publication may be reproduced, stored in or introduced into a retrieval system, or transmitted, in any form, or by any means (electronic, mechanical, photocopying, recording, or otherwise), without the prior written permission of the copyright owner.
Published in Great Britain by Dorling Kindersley Limited

A catalog record for this book
is available from the Library of Congress.
ISBN 978-0-5939-5934-3

DK books are available at special discounts when purchased in bulk for sales promotions, premiums, fund-raising, or educational use.
For details, contact: DK Publishing Special Markets,
1745 Broadway, 20th Floor, New York, NY 10019
SpecialSales@dk.com

Printed and bound in China

www.dk.com

This book was made with Forest Stewardship Council™ certified paper—one small step in DK's commitment to a sustainable future. Learn more at www.dk.com/uk/information/sustainability

CONTENTS

4	Dear little artists
6	Let's warm-up!
8	Spot the shape
10	Mark making
12	Pen pals
14	Colored materials
16	The color wheel
18	**Pippa's Pets**
19	Jessie the cat
20	Cilla the chicken
22	Buzz the bunny
23	Caramel the guinea pig
24	Hugo the hamster
25	Millie the mouse
26	Henrietta the duckling
28	Winter the dog
30	**Wild Animals**
31	Leaping lemur
32	Gentle giraffe

34	Sleepy sloth		64	Smart sheep
36	Enormous elephant		66	Perky pig
38	Champion cheetah		68	Lovely llama
39	Tough tiger		69	Adorable alpaca
40	Radical reptiles			
42	Wonderful wallaby		**70**	**Forest Friends**
44	Mischievous monkey		71	Funny frog
			72	Busy beaver
46	**Under the Sea**		74	Sneaky squirrel
47	Timid turtle		75	Happy hedgehog
48	Outstanding octopus		76	Creepy-crawlies
50	Playful penguin		78	Dashing deer
52	Fantastic fish		80	Brilliant birds
54	Jazzy jellyfish		82	Furry fox
55	Small starfish		84	Brown bear
56	Diving dolphin		86	Paw prints
57	Savvy shark			
			88	Fun formulas
58	**Farm Animals**		92	Time for color!
59	Grumpy goat		94	Index
60	Dazzling donkey		96	Acknowledgments
61	Huge horse			
62	Curious cow			

Dear little ARTISTS

When I was little, I discovered my love for drawing. The feel of crayons on paper, the sound of charcoal against board, and the different lines created by pencils have always fascinated me. It's magical how just a few lines can bring ideas, stories, and images to life on a blank page. From simple squiggles, I could create birds, sea creatures, and forest friends. I've learned some special techniques for drawing animals, and I can't wait to share them with you.

Our amazing planet Earth is home to a diverse array of fascinating animals, each with their own unique qualities. In this book, you will discover fun facts and explore new ways to draw. The book is organized into different sections: the first part focuses on how to sketch some of my family pets, and then we will learn to draw wild, sea, farm, and woodland animals.

So, are you ready to grab your pencils and sketchbook and embark on a wonderful drawing adventure?

I am looking forward to sharing this artistic journey with you!

Warmest and best,

Pippa xx

Let's WARM-UP!

Before I teach you to draw, we need to loosen up and get creative. Grab a pencil and some paper and try out these fun activities!

Draw a scribble over your page and see what animals you can make from it!

Blindfolded drawing

Put a blindfold on and see if you can draw a farm animal without looking—no peeking! When you're done, take off your blindfold and see how your drawing turned out.

TIP
If you don't have a blindfold, use a scarf or sweater to cover your eyes!

Opposite hand drawing

Pick a animal from the woods and then use the hand you don't use to write with to draw it on your page. Was that easy or difficult to draw?

See what different animals you and your friends can draw!

Air draw

Think of a wild animal. Then, use your finger to draw the animal in the air. Can your friends guess what it is?

Take a line for a walk

Starting at the top of the page, move your pencil around and don't lift it off until you reach the bottom. Try drawing different types of lines, such as wavy and loopy lines.

Spot the SHAPE

You might not believe me, but did you know that you can draw anything using simple shapes and letters? You just need to learn how to break things down! Learning to do this will make drawing so much easier and will help you to become a confident artist in no time!

TIP
The shapes you draw do not have to be perfect or even the same size as each other!

Basic shapes

Whether it's a triangle for a beak or a circle for the head, all animals can be broken down into basic shapes. Can you see any of these shapes in the animals on the next page?

Letters

Letters can also be used when drawing, for example we can use **W** shapes when drawing claws, and ears could be **C** shapes. See what letters you can spot on the next page!

A B C D E F G H
I J K L M N O P Q R
S T U V W X Y Z

Lines

There are long and short lines, thick and thin lines, straight and curved lines, and lines that can be wavy or curly. Each type of line can be used to add different textures to our drawings.

Horizontal

Vertical

Slanted

Wiggly

Zigzag

Loopy

Lines will vary in thickness depending on which part of the pencil you use. The tip creates thin lines but the side draws thicker ones.

Mark MAKING

In this book, we will use all kinds of lines and marks, from dots and dashes to squiggles and scallops. Let's practice drawing different marks to improve our drawing skills.

This guinea pig is made from lines, dots, and dashes.

TIP
Make sure you do your shading in pencil!

Marks

Marks, such as dots and dashes, might seem small but can be used in so many ways. A simple dot can transform into an eye, short dashes into claws, and some curls into fur.

Dots

Dashes

Vertical dashes

Curls

Scallops

Spots

Marks can add texture, like these scallops on the starfish.

10

SHADING

Shading makes your drawings look more realistic. This rectangle shows the different levels of shading, from dark to light. There are also various types of shading, all of which will give your animals texture. Why don't you try out some of these marks?

The vertical lines on this cat make it look scared.

The tight scribbles on this guinea pig make it look fluffy.

Ballpoint pens

Ballpoint pens have sticky ink. You can apply different amounts of pressure, making your lines darker and lighter. They are used for adding detail, but be careful not to smudge the marks they make.

Markers

Markers are a thick pen full of ink and come in many colors. They are great for adding texture and color to a drawing.

Pencils

With a pencil, you can create lots of different lines and techniques such as crosshatching and scribbling. If you make a mistake, you can use an eraser to easily erase it and start over.

Fine-tipped markers

Fine-tipped pens can come with smaller size tips. They are smooth to draw with and add texture to your art.

Fountain pens

These pens have a fancy tip called a nib that the ink flows through easily. Fountain pens are great for sketching.

Pen PALS

There are so many different materials you can use to create pictures—from simple things like sticks dipped in mud, to markers and pencils. As you try out different materials, you'll find the ones you like best for making your pictures.

TIP
You don't always have to use a black pen. Try using other colors, too!

Pick your tool

Sometimes you may want to draw, but you won't have any materials. Don't worry, you can draw with anything, from a stick in the mud to your finger in the sand!

Chalks

Chalks are soft and crumbly in texture, and are great for smudging and blending. They are smooth and easy to hold, making them fun to use for art activities.

TIP
Remember to wear old clothes, or wear an apron over your outfit to keep clean.

Colored MATERIALS

Adding color to your drawings can be really fun and messy. You can use colorful pastels, bright crayons, or even watercolor paint to help bring your creation to life. Each material can add something different to your drawings, whether that's detail or texture—let's explore the options!

Pastels

Pastels are like supersoft crayons, and are perfect for adding details. They come in all kinds of beautiful colors, and you can blend them together to make new colors, too.

Paints

Using paint is a lot of fun! You can use different types of paints, such as watercolor or acrylic, to create various effects, and different sizes of paintbrushes to make brushstrokes on the page.

Watercolor paint is great for backgrounds.

Crayons

Wax crayons are magical because they can't mix with water at all. When you use them on paper, they go on so smooth, and leave behind the brightest colors. They're great for adding detail to drawings.

Pencils

Pencils come in all colors, each with a smooth tip. You can mix and match colors to create textures and bring your animal creations to life on the page.

Keep the lids on your felt-tip pens to stop them from drying out!

Felt-tip pens

These pens come in a range of colors, with thick or thin tips. This makes them great for coloring big areas as well as adding detail.

The COLOR wheel

Colors are in the sky, in the flowers, everywhere! This circle is called the color wheel and it shows all the colors that we can see. These are the main colors that we mix to make all the other colors around us.

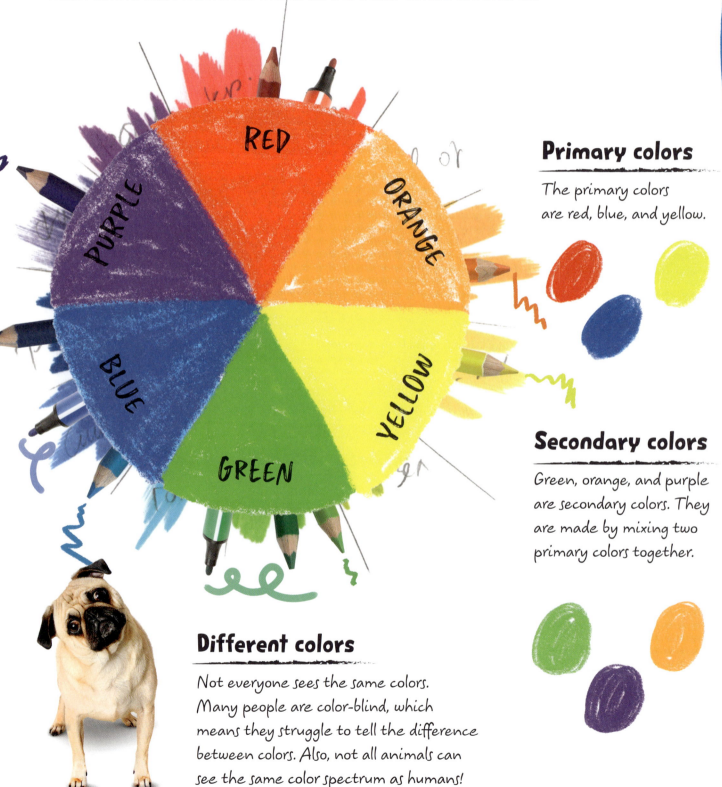

Primary colors

The primary colors are red, blue, and yellow.

Secondary colors

Green, orange, and purple are secondary colors. They are made by mixing two primary colors together.

Different colors

Not everyone sees the same colors. Many people are color-blind, which means they struggle to tell the difference between colors. Also, not all animals can see the same color spectrum as humans!

Mixing COLORS

RED + YELLOW = ORANGE

YELLOW + BLUE = GREEN

BLUE + RED = PURPLE

There are more colors than those on this color wheel, such as pink, teal, brown, white, and black. Each of these colors is made by mixing different amounts of the primary and secondary colors together. It's amazing how many colors we can make!

PINK   TEAL

BLACK — Adding black to a color makes it darker, and adding white makes it lighter.

WHITE

BROWN — Red, blue, and yellow mixed together make brown.

Contrasting colors

Contrasting colors are pairs of colors that sit opposite each other on the color wheel, for example red and green. When we use these colors in drawings, they go well together!

Contrasting colors can be found in nature too, just like on this chameleon.

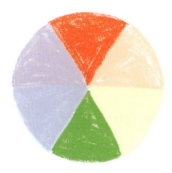
RED AND GREEN

PURPLE AND YELLOW

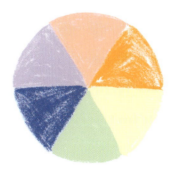
BLUE AND ORANGE

17

Pippa's
PETS

Do you have a furry friend at home?
Maybe a lovable dog, a cuddly cat,
a fluffy rabbit, or a playful hamster?
Would you like to learn how to draw them?

In this section, you will meet some of my
pets and I'll show you how to sketch them
using simple steps and capture their
cute personalities.

Jessie the CAT

My house is full of pets, including Jessie the cat. She loves to pounce, swat, and chase balls of soft wool—which sometimes gets her a bit tangled up. Let's draw her!

Jessie having lunch

1 Start by drawing a **V** shape for the head and then add two small upside-down **V** shapes on top for the ears.

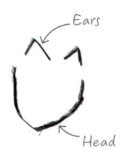

2 Next, draw a backward stretched **C** shape for the cat's body.

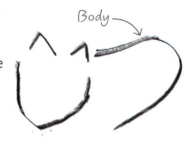

3 Draw two **C** shapes for the front paws—one is longer than the other. For the back legs, draw one sock shape and a letter **L**. Finish off by adding a long, thin tail.

4 Add some details to the face by drawing two triangles and dots for the eyes, a **Y** for the nose, lines for whiskers, and scribbles in the ears.

5 Finally, add some stripes and scribble a ball of wool for Jessie to chase!

TIP
Drawing a ball of wool is supereasy! Just scribble in a circle shape and add a long, wavy line.

19

Cilla the CHICKEN

Cilla and me sketching in the backyard

We have a lovely chicken family that lives in our backyard, including two hens, Cilla and Ginger, who are currently sitting on eggs in the chicken coop! We also have a really noisy rooster who starts crowing first thing every morning! Cilla loves to watch me sketch so it's about time we draw her...

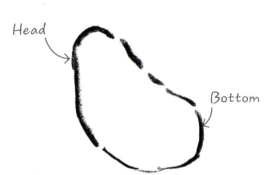

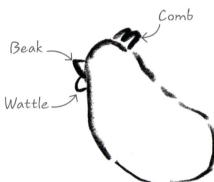

1 First, we will start off with a jelly-bean shape. This will be the chicken's body.

2 Add a letter **M** for the comb. Then, draw the letter **V** turned on its side for the beak and a **C** for the wattle.

TIP
You can put the dot in the eye wherever you want — it will just change which way the chicken is looking!

3 Next, add a circle and a dot for the eye. Draw a wavy shape for the tail feathers, and two lines with dashes for the legs and feet.

Chick this out!

Here's another fun fact... chickens dream just like we do! They might dream of juicy berries, baby chicks, or maybe a scary fox!

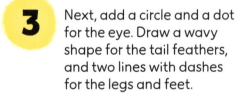

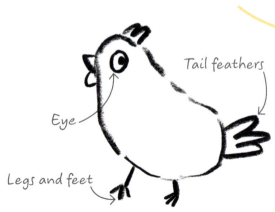

Get mucky, Clucky!

Chickens have an unusual way of keeping themselves clean—they take a dust bath! They roll around in dirt, shake it off, and then use their beaks to remove any excess dirt and dust.

The pattern, color, and arrangement of a bird's feathers is called a plumage.

4 Make a scribble underneath the feet for the shading and another for the wing.

5 Then, add scalloping for the feathers. They get a little bit bigger as you get farther away from the head.

TIP
Tilt the pencil on its side for a softer shading effect.

6 Finally, add a bit of shading with a gray pencil. This will help give some texture to the feathers.

Buzz the BUNNY

Buzz daydreaming

Rabbits love hugs and company, especially my bunny Buzz. If he isn't hopping around the yard with his sister, Annabella, he is sitting in my lap, daydreaming.

1 Draw a round potato shape for the head. Add a banana and scribble for each ear.

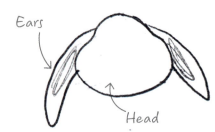

Ears · Head

2 Add a loop on its head for fur, ovals with dots for eyes, and a **Y** for the nose and mouth.

Fur · Eyes · Nose and mouth

3 Add whiskers, long lines for the body, two backward **C** shapes for feet, and two socks for front legs. Don't forget a tail!

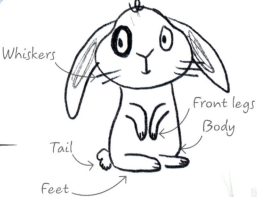

Whiskers · Front legs · Body · Tail · Feet

4 To finish it off, add your shading. Perfect!

Bunny binky!

When bunnies are really happy—full of the joys of spring—they hop, skip, jump, and sometimes perform a little twist in the air, known as a binky!

TIP Press down hard to make markings—like I've done around his eye!

22

Caramel the GUINEA PIG

Our Abyssinian guinea pigs are named Cookie and Caramel. They love to be hand-fed pieces of fruit and veggies after a shampoo spa session! Let's sketch one of my pampered pets, Caramel!

Cookie and Caramel

1 Start with a **V** shape for the head. Add a **U** shape for the nose, a round eye, and whiskers.

2 Draw two **W** shapes for little claws. Then add two small upside-down **V** shapes with scribbles inside to make ears.

3 For the hair, draw lots and lots of quick lines. They're very hairy!

4 Then, add your shading—lots of it on the body, and a little around the face.

Popcorning

When guinea pigs are excited they can "popcorn." This is when they jump up in the air, and sometimes they do a twist, too.

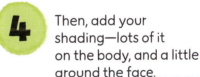

23

Hugo snacking

Hugo the HAMSTER

Meet Hugo, the cutest but greediest hamster you will ever come across. He loves nothing better than stuffing his cheeks with treats, and when he takes a sand bath he tosses his little legs in the air, just like a breakdancer. Let's draw him!

1 Draw a potato shape for the body. Then, add two **C** shapes for the little ears.

2 Next, draw two dots for eyes, a dot for the nose, and whiskers.

3 Now, let's add some **W** shapes for tiny paws.

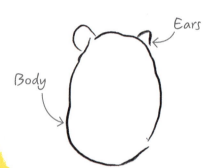

4 Finally, draw some scribbles for the fluffy fur and add some color.

TIP
Add a little scribble to the ears to give them a furry texture.

Stuff their cheeks

Some hamsters' cheeks can expand to nearly triple their size, so they can save snacks for later!

24

Millie the MOUSE

This is Millie—our adorable pet mouse! She is playful and loves to explore. She's always on the move, whether it's across your tummy, up your arm, or down your leg! Let's draw my squeaky little friend.

Millie smiling

1 Start by drawing a **V** for the head and two **C** shapes for the ears.

2 Next, draw a big **C** shape for the body and a long, thin tail.

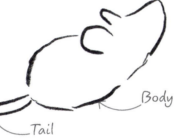

3 Draw a little dash for the eye, a dot for the nose, and whiskers. Don't forget some lines with dashes for Millie's paws, too!

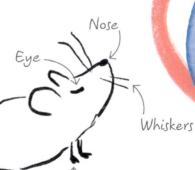

Tight squeeze

Mice don't have collarbones, so they can squeeze through tiny openings.

4 Are you ready to add some detail? Try drawing some squiggles for the fur and shading for texture.

TIP
Add some lines to the tail to make it more realistic.

25

Henrietta the DUCKLING

Henrietta is a crested runner duckling with a tuft of feathers on her head. She likes waddling around and splashing in the stream. Shall we draw her?

Henrietta chatting

Quack? Waap! Honk!

Ducks quack in different accents, depending on whether they are from the city or the country. Their sounds include quack quack, waap waap, and honk honk!

1 First, draw a circle for the head and add a little triangle for the beak. Don't forget to add a dot for the eye and one for the nose, too.

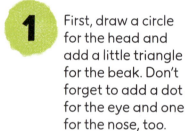

2 Next, draw a jelly-bean shape for the body and add a scribble for the wing.

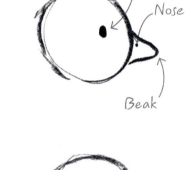

3 For the feet, draw two triangles, each with a line down the middle to make them look webbed.

Ducklings

Baby ducks are called ducklings, and they are born soft and fuzzy. Before hatching, they talk to each other with little cheeps.

Paddling crew

Ducks have a special oil, which they spread on their feathers, to make themselves waterproof so they can swim and dive easily. When they are in the water, they form a group to take care of each other—how cute!

NOW TRY...

Runner duck

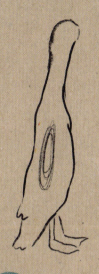

1 Draw a long bottle shape for the body with a scribble for the wing.

2 For the legs and feet, draw two block letter **L** shapes.

3 Add a triangle beak and a round eye. Now, add shading, and you're done!

4 Finally, add a scribble on the top of the head and scallops on the tummy for feathers.

Feathers

QUACK QUACK QUACK QUACK

Feathers

TIP
To make your duck look even more realistic, add some shading.

Ducks have webbed feet to help them swim fast.

27

Winter the DOG

Winter in the backyard

Meet my furry friend, Winter! She's a cute bichon frise who loves going on long hikes and snuggling up by the fire with a treat. She's the best companion I could ask for!

1 Start by drawing a circle for the head. Then, add two long, scribbly shapes for ears and a wobbly, scribbly line for the fringe.

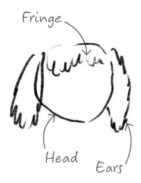

2 Next, sketch two scribbly **U** shapes to create the front legs and an **L** for the back leg. Then, draw two little dots for the eyes.

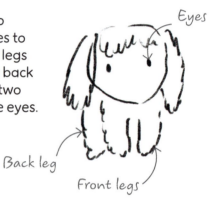

3 Now, add a scribbly tail, a dot, and a wavy line for the nose and mouth, and lots of little lines for the furry whiskers.

4 Finally, add some scribbles and paint for shading. There it is—a cute and fluffy bichon frise!

Same but different

Dogs come in all shapes and sizes. Some are tall and some are short, some are fluffy and some have no hair!

WOOF WOOF

How are you feeling?

Dogs tell us how they feel through barks and body language, using their eyes, tail, nose, and shoulders to communicate with their human friends. When they're happy, they show it by jumping, smiling, licking, and wagging their tail.

NOW TRY...

Poodle

1 Draw three scribbly ovals to create the fluffy head and ears. Then, add a big **V** for the chin.

2 Draw two lines for the chest, a jelly-bean body, a tail with a pom-pom on the end, and dots for the nose, mouth, and eyes.

3 Add four legs with scribbly circles for the fluffy ankles and **W** shapes for paws.

4 Finally, shade or color in your drawing, and you have a poodle!

Pointer puppy

1 Draw a triangle for the head. Add dots for the eyes and a dot and line for the nose and mouth.

2 Next, draw two scribbles for the ears and two **U** shapes for the paws.

3 Use scribbles to make a furry body. Add a scribble for the tail, too.

4 Finish off your dog however you like. You can add a patch around the eye, whiskers, or shading.

Wild ANIMALS

Are you ready to sketch some awesome critters? Our planet is full of amazing animals. Some run at superfast speeds like cheetahs, while others move slowly like sloths. Some are bouncy like kangaroos, while others just lumber along like elephants. Each animal has its unique way to move!

Are you ready to let your creativity run wild and sketch some of the coolest critters out there? In this section, I'm going to walk you through simple steps to sketch some of your favorite wild animals. So, grab your pencils, let's get started, and have some fun.

Leaping LEMUR

Have you ever seen lemurs? They look amazing with their black-and-white striped tails. These little guys love to leap, climb, and bounce around. Did you know they can dance and sing? Can you draw a little lemur?

1 Begin by drawing a triangle shape for the head, and draw two eyes. Add two diamond shapes for eye patches and color them in black.

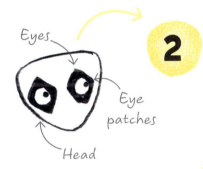

2 Next, add a squarish nose and a tiny dash for the mouth. Then, draw two long lines for the lemur's arms. Don't forget the ears!

3 Let's make the legs by drawing two arches for the knees and some dashes for the pointy toes.

4 Time for the fun part—draw a long, curved, striped tail!

5 Finally, for the finishing touch, add some scribbles and shading to give your lemur fur.

Lemurs hold their tails up as a warning to rival lemurs.

TIP You can also add a tuft of hair to your lemur!

31

Tower

Did you know that a group of giraffes is called a tower? This is because they are so tall that they tower over other animals!

TIP
Make sure you start your drawing at the top of the page so that you have enough space.

Gentle GIRAFFE

Giraffes are the tallest animals in the world. They have elegant long necks, horns called ossicones, and a patterned coat. They are herbivores, which means that they only eat leaves, fruit, and berries. Let's draw this gentle giraffe.

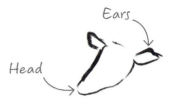

1 Start by drawing a triangle with rounded corners for the head and two small diamonds for the ears.

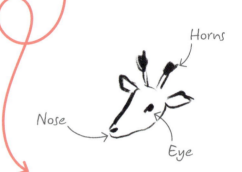

2 Next, draw two horns with black scribbles on top. Then, add two dots—one for the eye and one for the nose.

3 For the body, draw a funny-looking sock shape. Then, add two lines with a scribble at the end for the tail.

TRY THIS!

Try experimenting with different line thicknesses. First, try drawing the head of a giraffe by pressing lightly, and then press down harder. Thicker lines can make your drawing really stand out!

LIGHT PRESSURE

HARD PRESSURE

Tongue

Not only do Giraffes have long necks, they also have long blue tongues that they use to reach tall branches.

Patches

No two giraffes have the same pattern. Each pattern is unique like a fingerprint.

Hooves

Legs

4 Now, add four long, thin cucumbers for the legs.

5 Finally, scribble in some patches for the pattern and add some shading. Don't forget to color the hooves in black. Wow, look at your giraffe!

1 Let's start by drawing an oval shape for the head, a banana for one of the arms and a hook for the other.

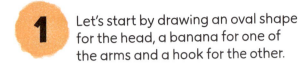
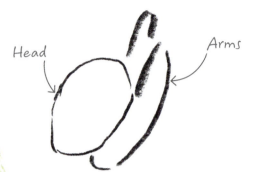

2 Next, add dots for the eyes and nose, and a wiggly mouth. Then draw a curve around each eye.

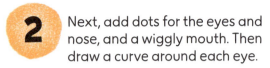
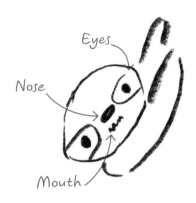

Sleepy SLOTH

Did you know that sloths are believed to be the slowest mammals on Earth? They are so slow that algae and fungi grow on their fuzzy fur—that's why it sometimes looks a bit green! Sloths are in no hurry to get anywhere and are usually found sleeping. Are you ready to draw a sleepy sloth?

Swimming

Despite being so slow, sloths are actually good swimmers. They can swim three times faster than they can move on land, with help from their long arms and legs.

Cecropia leaves

While they don't eat much, sloths like to munch on cecropia leaves. Let's draw them...

1   **2**

3

34

3 Now, add a big curve for the body with two cucumber shapes for the other arms. Remember to add little claws, too.

Claws — Legs — Body

Sloths only have two or three claws on their front feet.

Hanging around

Sloths spend most of their time just hanging around and sleeping in trees. They can sleep for roughly 15 hours, and even when they are awake, they barely move!

4 Let's add some scribbles and shading for fur!

Fur

A sloth's fur contains algae, which helps camouflage it in trees.

5 Finally, draw two long lines between the arms to make a branch to hang off. Add some leaves if you'd like, too!

Branch

1 Start by drawing a big potato shape for the body.

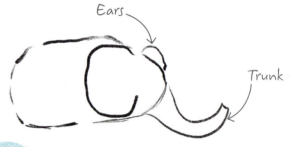

2 For the trunk, draw a backward block letter **J**. Next, add a big **C** for one ear, and a small upside-down **U** for the other.

3 Now, let's draw four vase shapes for the legs. Don't forget a **J** for the cute tail!

Swimming trunks?

Elephants are strong swimmers. They use their legs to help them move and their trunks as a snorkel!

Enormous ELEPHANT

Elephants are the largest living land animals, and are absolutely spectacular. They have large ears and a long nose called a trunk. They use their trunk for all kinds of things such as eating, trumpeting, and playing. Let's get drawing!

TIP Make sure you draw this one in pencil so that you can erase bits of it!

Follow the leader!

Did you know that a baby elephant will often hold onto its mother's tail with its trunk? This is for comfort, and so that it doesn't get lost—how sweet!

An elephant's wrinkles help it stay cool by trapping moisture.

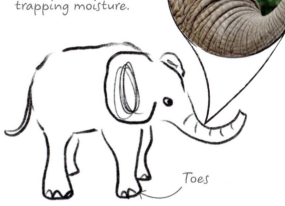

4 Erase the line across the face and add an eye.

5 Let's draw some bumpy, wavy lines for the toes and scallops on the trunk. Add a scribble in the ear, too.

6 Finish by adding some shading to make the elephant's skin look wrinkled! Perfect!

1 First, draw a circle for the head with two **C** shapes for the little ears.

2 Now, draw a jelly-bean snout, an upside-down **Y** for the mouth, and two dots for eyes. Add a scribbly tuft of fur and some markings.

3 Draw two curved lines for the body. Add two straight front legs and two bent-back legs. Draw four round circles with little dashes for the paws and a banana for the tail.

Champion
CHEETAH

Cheetahs are known for their speed and spots. Their spotted coats help them blend into their surroundings when hunting. Quickly, let's draw!

Superspeedy

Cheetahs can run up to 75 mph (120 kph), making them the fastest animal on land. They could beat Usain Bolt in a race!

4 Decorate the body with scribbled circles for the spots. Finish off with light scribbles and shading.

TIP
Avoid adding too many spots to your cheetah's face — they could cover up the features!

Tough TIGER

Now this is a BIG cat! Tigers are fierce and powerful hunters, and they are the largest wildcat in the world. But all cats like to play, and these tough tigers are no exception. Let's get drawing!

1 First, draw a rounded triangle for the head and two small **C** shapes for the ears. Next, add a potato shape for the body.

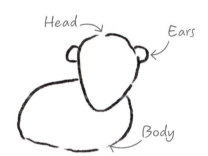

2 Draw a sock shape for the back leg and two curvy cucumbers for the front legs.

Swimming

Most cats hate water, but not tigers. In fact, they love swimming and are very good at it!

3 Add a curved tail. Then, draw the eyes, two lines for the markings, and a letter **Y** for the nose. Add some dots around the nose, too.

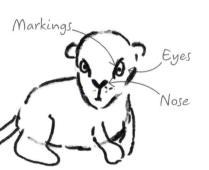

4 Scribble in some stripes for the tiger's coat and some small dashes for the claws on the paws. Add whiskers, and then get coloring!

Radical REPTILES

Reptiles have existed for hundreds of millions of years and were even around before the dinosaurs! They are cold-blooded and scaly animals that are found on land and in water.

Are you ready to draw these scaly critters?

Nile crocodile

Palm gecko

Panther chameleon

Crocodile 1

These predators are the largest reptiles in the world. They have a strong bite, so watch out!

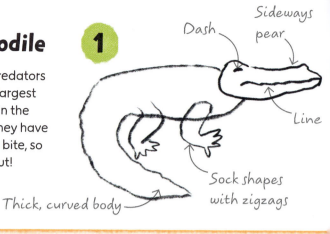

Dash — Sideways pear — Line — Sock shapes with zigzags — Thick, curved body

Gecko 1

These small lizards love warm places. Geckos mostly come out at night and can come in lots of colors.

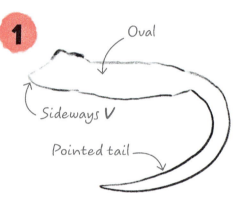

Oval — Sideways V — Pointed tail

Chameleon 1

Chameleons seem magical—they can change color to blend in with their surroundings!

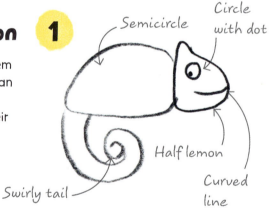

Semicircle — Circle with dot — Half lemon — Curved line — Swirly tail

Snake 1

These reptiles don't have legs or arms. Instead, they like to slither. Some can be venomous— be careful!

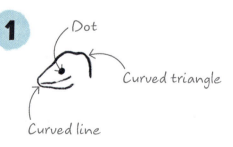

Dot — Curved triangle — Curved line

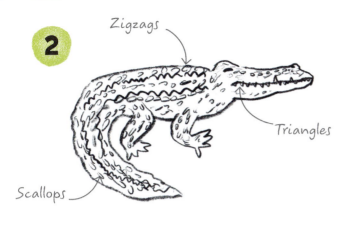

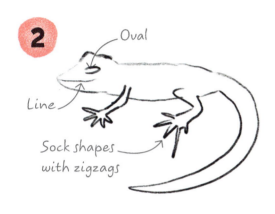
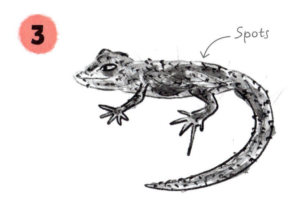

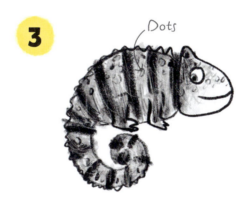

Red spitting cobra

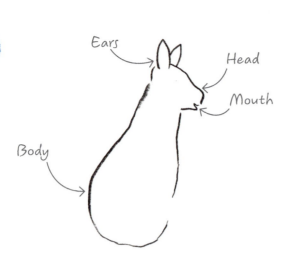
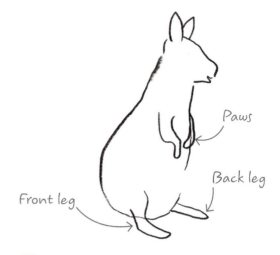

1 First, draw a pear shape for the body. Then, add an almond shape for the head and two leaf shapes for the ears. You can add a tiny sideways **V** for the mouth, too!

2 Next, sketch three floppy sock shapes for the front leg and paws, and a long stretched **U** for the back leg.

Wonderful
WALLABY

Most people have heard of kangaroos, but did you know that there are smaller, similar animals called wallabies? Female wallabies carry their young, called joeys, in a cosy pouch. Let's draw a mommy wallaby and her joey.

Wallabies love to eat grasses and plants, like ferns.

A hop, skip, and jump

Wallabies are known to jump. They can hop at speeds of up to 30 mph (50 kph). Wallabies can also crawl and swim!

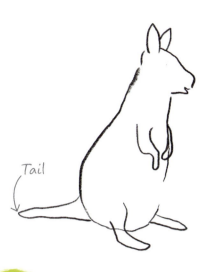

3 It's time to add the tail. Draw a long sideways **V** shape.

4 For the cute little joey in the pouch, draw a sock shape for the head and a leaf shape for the ear. Now, add two tiny **W** shapes for the paws.

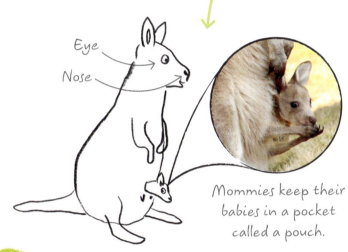

Mommies keep their babies in a pocket called a pouch.

5 Let's give the mommy and joey faces. Draw two circles with dots for the eyes, two small dashes for their noses, and two little ovals to finish the ears.

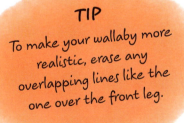

TIP
To make your wallaby more realistic, erase any overlapping lines like the one over the front leg.

6 Don't forget to paint in some texture for the fuzzy fur. This will make your wallaby look even more cuddly and cute.

43

TIP
Don't worry if your monkey's head isn't a perfect circle!

Mischievous
MONKEY

Monkeys are supersmart animals, and are great at problem-solving. They live in groups where they take care of each other. They love to chatter and spend their time swinging from tree to tree.

1 Start by drawing a circle for the monkey's head and two small **C** shapes for the ears.

2 Add two circles with dots for the eyes and a wavy line for the forehead. Then, add a **Y** shaped nose with a dash for the mouth.

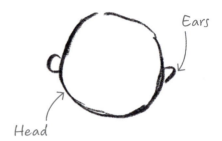

Monkeys love nuts. Many use tools to break open the shells.

3 Draw two curvy lines for the arms and two arches for the knees. Add zigzags at the end of the arms and knees for hands and feet. Then, draw lines from the hands to the feet to finish the legs.

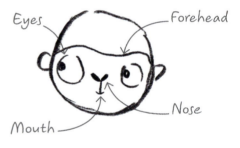

Carry me!

Many monkeys will carry their babies on their backs to keep them safe, and to stop them from getting lost!

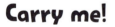

44

TRY THIS!

Sleeping monkey

1 Draw a bean shape for the body, two **C** shapes for the ears, and a small oval for the face. Add four dashes for eyes and eyebrows, a line for the mouth, and two dots for the nose.

2 Next, sketch in two teardrop shapes for the legs and a long banana shape for the arm. Add zigzags for the hands and feet.

3 Finally, add some scribbles and paint for the furry texture of the monkey.

Hanging around

Monkeys love to swing in the trees. They grab branches with their hands, feet, and sometimes even their tail!

5 Finally, add some shading to really bring your monkey to life. Don't forget to add a loopy scribble for a tuft of fur!

4 Draw a long, curvy tail. Then, add a couple of scribbles for fur.

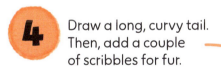

Tail

Tuft of fur

45

Under the SEA

Let's embark on an exciting journey into the enchanting world of sea creatures! From mysterious, inky octopuses to dangerous, hungry sharks, we'll explore the ocean together.

In this section, I'll show you how to draw some of your favorite animals of the deep-blue sea. So... let's dive right in!

Timid TURTLE

Turtles have a hard shell that covers their body just like a snail, and they can live both in the water and on land. They move slowly and steadily on land, but move much quicker through the water. Here's how you draw these beautiful animals.

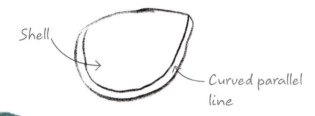

1 Start by drawing the shell, which is a semicircle with a curved parallel line around the edge.

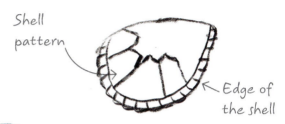

2 Next, draw some house shapes on the shell to make a cool pattern. Then, add scalloping around the edge of the shell.

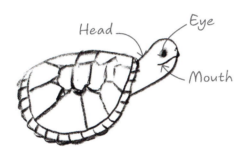

3 Now, draw a peanut shape for the head. Add a dot for the eye and a curved line for the mouth. Don't forget to finish the pattern of the shell, too.

4 Next, draw a banana shape for the front flipper and add two wavy lines for the flippers at the back.

5 Sketch and scribble in some circles for the turtle's skin, and add some shading to your drawing. It looks great!

TIP
Use harder pencil strokes on the shell to give it texture.

47

1 Start by drawing a bell shape for the head.

2 Next, draw eight curved lines or long **S** shapes for the arms.

Head

Arms

Outstanding
OCTOPUS

Did you know that octopuses are like underwater magicians? They can change into different colors to hide, squirt out black ink to scare away attackers, and fit into small spaces, which is amazing since they have eight long arms. Let's learn how to draw these fabulous sea animals.

Octopus ink irritates predators' eyes.

Armed and ready

Octopuses have two rows of suckers running up and down each of their eight arms. They use them to smell, taste, grab, and attach to things.

48

3 Complete the arms by drawing another curved line from the tip of one arm to the beginning of the next one.

Tip
Beginning of next arm

4 Draw scallops on the underside of all eight arms to represent the suckers, and add dots for eyes.

Eyes
Suckers

Beat that!

Did you know that an octopus has three hearts? One moves blood around the body, and the other two pump blood through the gills. Also, their blood is blue!

5 Finally, scribble in some shading with your pencil or paint. Well done!

TIP
Draw some dots on the head of your octopus to make his skin look rubbery.

49

Baby, it's cold outside

Adults and their chicks huddle together to keep warm, but they don't stand still. Instead, penguins will shuffle around and take turns being on the outside of the group, where it is coldest.

Playful PENGUIN

There are 18 species of penguins, and these black-and-white birds move in lots of funny ways! They bob and waddle, walk and run, bounce and belly flop, and when they want to go really fast, they slide on their tummies! Ready? Let's draw our playful pal!

1 To draw a penguin, draw a bean shape for the body and a triangle for the beak.

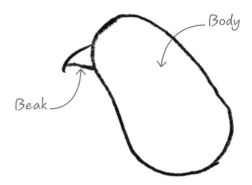

2 Draw a sock shape for the front flipper and a triangle for the back one. Add a dot for the eye, too.

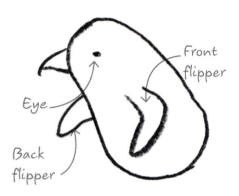

3 Now, draw a scribbly **W** for the tail. Add three backward **L** shapes for the legs and join the ends together with curved lines to make the feet webbed.

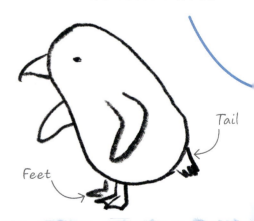

50

Small singers

While penguins are not songbirds, some species have been known to "sing" to talk to other penguins in their group, attract females, and defend their space.

NOW TRY...

Rockhopper penguin

1 Draw a pear shape for the penguin's body.

2 Add two small dots for the eyes and a small triangle for the beak. Add a curved line for the belly, too. On the head, draw some spiky feathers.

3 Draw two wings on the side and two **W** shapes for webbed feet at the bottom. Then, add some shading.

4 Finally, it's time to scribble in some shading for the furry texture.

Penguins have a layer of air under their feathers to help them float.

TIP
Add some ice around your penguin using a blue or light-purple color.

Fantastic FISH

Fish come in all different colors, shapes, sizes, and patterns. Some like to swim alone while others swim together in groups called schools. Here, I will show you how to draw a variety of fantastic fish...

Panther grouper

Microcanthus

Spotted fish

The panther grouper has lots of beautiful black spots on its body. It is a big fish that can be found in clear, tropical waters.

1 Draw a lemon shape for the body. Add a spiky fin on top, three fins near the tummy, and a spiky tail. Draw an eye, too!

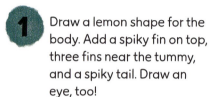

2 Draw in spots all over the fish. Then, add some lines to its fins for texture.

3 To really bring your spotted fish to life, add some shading.

Striped fish

The microcanthus has beautiful black-and-yellow stripes. It loves company so it swims in a school.

1 Draw a triangle for the body, with two triangular fins. Add a wavy tail, and a circle and a dot for the eye.

2 Let's add some stripes! Make your fish as striped as you want!

3 Finally, let's shade the fish in to make it look more realistic.

Puffer fish

Clown fish

Emperor angelfish

Puffer fish

The puffer is an amazing fish. When it feels scared, it fills its body with water and air to puff up and protect itself!

1 Draw a circle for the body and an **M** for the mouth. Draw a square fin and a wavy tail, and add some lines.

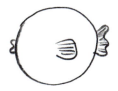

2 Add a circle with a dot for the eye. Then, draw lots of **V** shapes for the sharp and pointy spines.

3 Now, let's add some shading to make the skin and scales look rough.

Swirly fish

The angelfish has a swirly pattern and long, flowing fins that shimmer in the sunlight and look like wings.

1 Draw a shovel shape for the body, with a spike at the bottom and on one side. Add an oval with lines for the fin, and then draw an eye.

2 Draw some swirly patterns across the body and some lines on the tail and fin.

3 Shade in the body, leaving parts of the swirly pattern white to make it stand out!

Clown fish

The clown fish is a small orange fish that lives in coral reefs in warm waters.

1 Start by drawing an oval for the body. Add four little semicircles for the fins and a fan shape for the tail.

2 Next, draw one more fin, and then add lines to all the fins. Draw a dot for the eye and curvy lines across the body for the pattern.

3 To finish your drawing, add some scribbles and shading, or even some color!

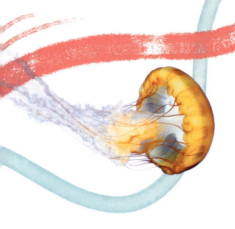

Jazzy JELLYFISH

Jellyfish are really cool sea creatures that look like floating umbrellas! They have a soft, jellylike body and long, wavy tentacles. Jellyfish drift gracefully through the ocean but don't be fooled, they can sting! Are you ready to draw a jazzy jellyfish?

1 Begin by drawing a semicircle for the body. Then, add a scalloped edge over the straight line.

Scalloped edge — Body

2 Next, draw three thick, wavy lines for the arms—these help a jellyfish move food up to its mouth.

Arms

3 Add in some shorter, thinner, wavy lines for the tentacles—these are for stinging!

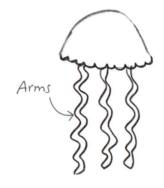

Tentacles

4 Finally, add some shading to finish your jellyfish.

TIP
Try doing the wavy lines of the arms without taking your pencil off the page.

Soft and squishy

Did you know that jellyfish don't have a brain, a heart, bones, or blood? That's why they're so jellylike!

Small STARFISH

While they are star shaped, starfish are not fish as their name suggests. They have tough, prickly skin to protect them from predators. Most starfish have five arms, and if one of their arms gets hurt they can regrow it!

1 First, draw a big star shape to give your starfish five long arms.

2 Then, add little **C** shapes on each arm for the bumpy, tough skin.

Arms

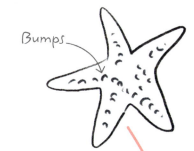
Bumps

3 You can also add some scribbles or shading to the arms to make it more detailed. And there you have it—a little starfish!

Little legs

Starfish have lots of tiny feet on their arms to help them move slowly along the ocean floor. Starfish fill their feet with water, which makes their arms move.

TIP
You can draw a star by using this template— make sure you erase the lines inside!

Start here

55

Diving DOLPHIN

Dolphins are friendly and supersmart animals. They can swim very fast, and they communicate using sounds like squeaks, trills, grunts, whistles, and clicks. They love to play and jump out of the water. Now it's your turn to draw a diving dolphin!

1 Draw a banana shape for the body. Next, draw a small cucumber for the beak and a dot for the eye.

2 Now, add on two sock shapes for the flippers.

3 Draw two curved lines and an **M** shape for the tail and a triangle for the dorsal fin. Don't forget to add a blowhole, too!

4 Add a line down the middle of the tail. Add some scribbles and shading and you're done!

We're in this together

Dolphins are social animals, and have close family connections. They travel in groups called pods, and work together to raise their young.

56

Savvy SHARK

Sharks are large and fast creatures of the sea! They have big, sharp teeth and huge jaws that they use to chomp and chew. They feed on fish, squid, seals, and even other sharks. Some like to go on solo missions, while others team up to find their prey. Here's how you draw a savvy shark.

1 Begin by drawing a large, stretched lemon shape for the body.

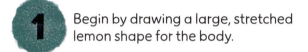

2 Next, draw seven triangles for all the fins—two on the top and five underneath. Add a dot for the eye and a curved line for the mouth. Draw some zigzags for the sharp teeth, too.

3 Draw a banana shape with a line across the middle for the shark's tail. Add three curved lines for the gills, too.

4 To finish your shark, add some shading and scribbles to make it more realistic. Good job!

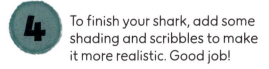

Sink your teeth into this!

Sharks have been around for more than 400 million years—long before dinosaurs. Unlike other animals, the only remains sharks leave behind are teeth, since they don't have bones!

Farm ANIMALS

Are you ready to explore the farm and learn how to draw your favorite animals?

In this section, you'll find step-by-step instructions on drawing clever pigs, magnificent horses, and all of their other farm friends. You'll also discover fun facts about each animal and colorful illustrations to inspire you.

Get your favorite sketching supplies ready, because it's time to embark on a drawing adventure with these lovable farm animals!

Grumpy GOAT

Most goats live in fields and on farms. They have soft fur and some have little horns on their heads. They are very playful and curious, and can jump really high! Have you ever drawn a cute goat?

1 Start by drawing a bean shape for the goat's body. Next, draw a small oval for the head.

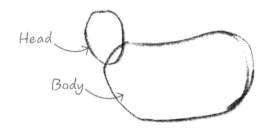

Cliff climbers

Some goats live on cliffs rather than in fields. These goats have special hooves to help them grip the rocks.

2 Draw two floppy ears, two circles with a line inside for the eyes, and a dash for the nose. Add an upside-down **T** for the mouth.

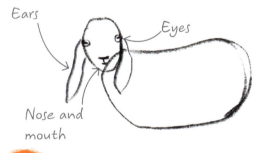

4 To make the goat look furry, add some shading and sketch a fuzzy tail. That looks great!

3 Now, draw four long sock shapes for the legs and scribbles for the hooves. Don't forget to draw some horns, too.

Dazzling DONKEY

Donkeys are strong, friendly animals that love to have their smooth coat petted. They like to eat fruit and are incredibly smart. Let's draw one together.

1 Start by drawing an upside-down pear shape for the head and two leaf shapes with black scribbles inside for the ears.

2 Next, draw a bean shape for the body and a cucumber for the tail.

3 Draw four long, curved rectangles for the legs. Add four scribbly hooves, too.

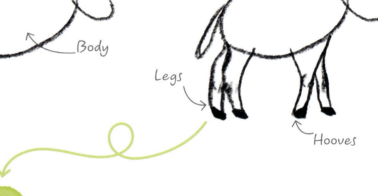

4 Now, sketch two dots for the eyes, two dashes for the nostrils, and a curved line for the nose. Remember to add some scribbles for the mane and fur, too.

Noisy bunch
Donkeys communicate by making "hee-haw" sounds to each other.

TIP Try out different markings on your donkey!

Huge HORSE

Horses are graceful animals with a beautiful, sleek coat. They have a long mane and tail that can be brushed and braided. Horses can be different colors and have long legs that help them run fast.

1 Begin by drawing a bean shape for the horse's body. Next, draw a teardrop shape for the long neck.

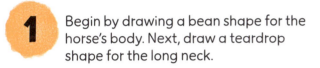

2 Add a bean shape for the head. Sketch two triangles for ears, a dash for the eye, and one for the nose.

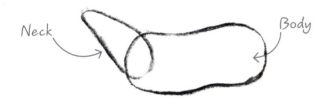

3 Draw three curved rectangles for the front legs and one of the back legs. For the other back leg, draw two triangles. Then add some scribbles for the bushy tail.

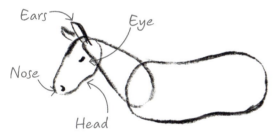

Born to run

Baby horses, or foals, can walk and run within a few hours of being born.

4 Add some shading to give the coat texture and sketch in a scribbled mane. Add some hooves, too. Wow!

61

1 Grab a pencil and sketch a large oval shape for the head and two leaf shapes for the ears.

2 Add a small oval with two dots inside for the nose and two dots for the eyes. Draw a large potato shape for the body. Then, add a curved line with three teardrops for the udder and two horns.

Have you herd this?

Cows are social animals who like to live in big groups. These groups are called herds.

3 Next, sketch four rectangles extending from the body for the legs. Draw a thin banana with a scribble at the end for the tail.

Curious COW

A cow is a big, gentle animal that you often see in the country. They like to eat grass and hay, and they talk to each other by mooing. Many cows have short fur with spots, while others have long, wavy fur. They make milk, which can be turned into cheese, butter, and ice cream!

Munching away

Cows are always hungry. They spend their time in fields eating lots of grass—this is called grazing.

Spots

4 Add the cow's spots and erase any unnecessary lines. Then, add some texture to your cow.

5 Finally, finish your drawing with ink or paint. Now you have a curious cow!

TIP
Try drawing patches on your cow instead of spots.

NOW TRY...

Highland cow

1 Scribble some lines for the fur. Add two half-banana shapes for horns and two **V** shapes for ears.

2 Add a small oval with two dashes for the nose and add scribbles around the nose.

3 For the body, draw two lines. Add two **U** shapes for legs.

4 Add an upside-down bottle for the back leg. Draw lots of scribbles for fur.

63

1 First, sketch a cloudlike circle for the head. Then, draw two dots for the eyes and a **Y** for the cute nose.

2 Next, draw in a small fluffy cloud for the top of the head. Then, add two **U** shapes for ears and two **V** shapes for horns.

TIP
Make sure you draw this sheep in pencil so that you can erase some bits.

3 Then, draw in a big cloud shape for the body.

Smart SHEEP

Sheep are fluffy animals with thick wool that can be made into warm sweaters and cosy blankets. They love eating grass and spending time in wide open fields with their friends. Let's draw a sheep!

Follow the leader

Sheep are social animals and they like to closely bond with each other. They like this so much, they will travel together in groups and often follow each other.

Sheep wool is spun into yarn, which is then used to make clothes.

NOW TRY...

Lamb

1 Draw a potato shape for the body, an oval for the head, and two leaf shapes for ears.

2 Draw three curved rectangles for legs and a triangle for the back leg. Add a little tail.

3 Add two dots for eyes, a heart for the nose, and an upside-down T for the mouth. Then, add scribbles for fur.

4 Now, draw four cloudlike rectangles for the legs.

5 Erase any extra lines. Then, using the side of your pencil, shade in the face and add wavy lines to make soft, woolly fur.

Legs

Sheep produce an oil called lanolin that is water resistant and protects sheep from the weather.

65

Perky PIG

Pigs have a cute snout, a curly tail, and can even be furry They love to play and roll around in the mud, which helps keep them cool and protected from the sun. They are friendly and talk to each other by making funny squeals and grunts. Pigs are very smart and can even learn to do tricks! Are you ready to draw?

Snuggly sleepover

Pigs love to be connected to each other, so they tend to sleep in a pile, all snuggled up.

1 Start by drawing a potato shape for the pig's body using a pencil.

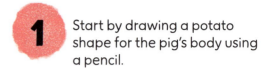

2 Then, draw a small oval and two tiny dots for the snout. Don't forget two dots for the eyes.

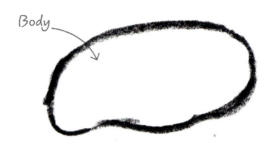

3 Now, add two V shapes for the ears. Then, add four legs by drawing four stretched-out triangles.

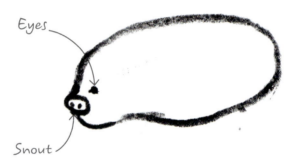

NOW TRY...

Piglet

1 Draw a bean shape for the body. Add a dot for the eye, an oval with two dots for the snout, and a backward **C** for the ear.

2 Add four rectangles for the legs. Don't forget a curly tail, too.

3 Now, add some scribbles for the fur and some shading to make your piglet more realistic.

4 Lastly, draw a curly tail and some spots and lines all over the pig's body to make it look cute and fuzzy.

TIP
Try using different colors on your pig.

Piglets

Pigs give birth to a group, or litter, of babies called piglets. Piglets love to run and explore, but they don't like to be too far away from their mother.

It's thought that some pigs have curly tails so that they don't get in the way during a fight.

Tail

Lovely LLAMA

Llamas have long necks and ears and soft fur, which can be clipped to make sweaters or woolly hats. Llamas are friendly, but watch out, because if they get upset, they might spit at you! Grab your pencil and let's draw!

Load me up!

Llamas can carry heavy loads, but if they are loaded with too much they'll sit down and refuse to move!

1 Begin by drawing a potato shape for the llama's body and an oval shape on top for the neck.

2 Draw an almond shape for the head and two **V** shapes for the ears. Add a dot for the eye and two dashes for the nose and mouth.

3 Draw four long sock shapes for the legs and add pointy black scribbles for the hooves. Don't forget a banana shape for the tail.

4 To make the llama look furry, draw some wavy lines and scribbles with your pencil. Beautiful!

Adorable ALPACA

Alpacas are long-necked, fluffy animals like llamas. Most alpacas live at high altitude in the South American Andes Mountains. They are gentle, friendly, inquisitive, and curious critters and some people even keep them as pets! Let's draw this adorable alpaca.

1 Draw a cloudlike oval for the body. Then, draw an upside-down woolly sock shape for the head.

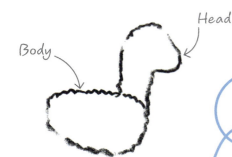

2 Draw two **V** shapes for ears, a teardrop tail, and dashes for the eye, nose, and mouth. Add a curved line for the snout.

3 For the legs, draw four fluffy rectangles. Don't forget some lines for hooves.

4 Add lots of wavy, scribbly lines to make your alpaca fluffy. Don't forget to give it a fuzzy hairdo, too.

Scream and shout

When there's danger alpacas scream, and when they're excited they make a hooting sound!

TIP
You can add shading to give your alpaca spots.

69

Forest
FRIENDS

There are lots of different animals that live in the forest. Some make their homes high up in the trees, some like to live in cosy dens, and others prefer to have secret burrows underground. Everywhere you look, you can see animals hopping, chasing, darting, or scrambling around as they have fun playing in the forest.

In this section, we're going to learn cool things about these awesome animals and how to draw them. So, what are we waiting for?

Funny FROG

Frogs are amphibians, and they live in water and on land. You can find them in yards, woods, and parks. They have smooth, moist skin and long back legs that help them jump, hop, and swim. Let me show you how to draw these funny critters!

1 First, start by drawing an oval for the frog's head. Next, add two circles to represent the eyes.

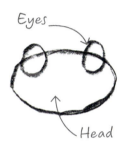

2 Inside each eye, draw smaller ovals for the pupils. Then, draw a curved line to create the mouth.

Small and sticky

A frog's foot is like a tiny flipper. It is webbed, which helps a frog swim and also gives it a good grip when hopping around.

3 Now, draw a curved line underneath the head for the body. Add four curved lines for legs. Don't forget to draw two webbed feet, too!

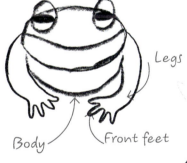

4 Add two **M** shapes at each side for the back feet. For a finishing touch, add spots and scribbles and shading on the frog's body.

71

Busy BEAVER

Beavers have thick brown fur and big teeth. Their big, flat tail helps them paddle in the water and stay steady on land. Did you know that beavers can hold their breath underwater for up to 15 minutes? How impressive! Let me show you how to draw our busy beaver.

1 Draw a rough circle for the head. Then, add two small, scribbled circles on top for the beaver's ears.

2 Next, draw two small dots for the eyes, an oval for the nose, and an upside-down **T** for the mouth. Don't forget to add whiskers, too.

Beaver builders

Beavers are nature's little engineers. They use their sharp teeth to chop down trees and build dams in the water.

3 Now, draw a big **U** shape for the beaver's body. For the tail, draw a long teardrop shape extending from the back of the body.

72

NOW TRY...

Dam

1 Dams are made of sticks. Draw a simple diagonal line to start your dam.

2 Add a few more lines that cross over each other.

3 Keep adding lines to complete your dam. Try adding some waves lines for water, too.

Big bite

Beavers have superstrong teeth that can gnaw through their favorite food—wood. Did you know their teeth are orange, too?

A beaver will slap its tail on the water as a sign of danger.

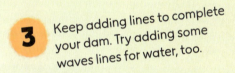

Arms

Feet

4 Draw two shell shapes with lines inside for the feet. Then, add two curved **V** shapes for the beaver's arms.

5 To make the beaver look furry, use your pencil to add shading by making quick scribbles.

1 Draw a bean shape for the squirrel's body and two, tiny party hats for the ears.

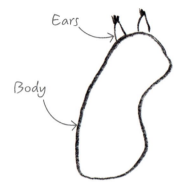

Sneaky
SQUIRREL

Squirrels are like little acrobats with bushy tails. They can climb trees and jump really far. They like to collect nuts and seeds to eat, and they have fluffy fur that keeps them warm. You might see squirrels in a park or even in a backyard!

2 Then, draw a dot and a curved line above it for the eye. Add a tiny **C** for the nose and two cucumber shapes for the feet.

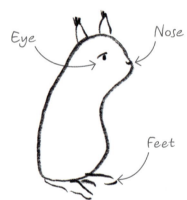

Twitchy tails

Squirrels talk to each other using sounds, but if they get angry or sense danger they twitch their tail to warn each other.

3 Now, lightly draw a bean shape facing the other way and scribble it in—this is the big bushy tail.

TIP
Use the side of your pencil for bold pencil lines, and use the tip for thinner lines.

4 Lastly, draw a curved line for the leg and two sock shapes for the arms. What a cute squirrel!

Happy HEDGEHOG

Hedgehogs are shy critters with little pointy spines all over their backs. When scared, hedgehogs roll up into a ball to defend themselves. They live on the ground but they can swim and climb, too! Let's draw a happy hedgehog!

1 Start by drawing a lemon shape for the body.

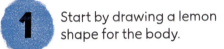

2 Next, draw an eye, a small dot for the nose, and two black circles for the ears. Add four thick but small **L** shapes for the legs.

3 Then, have fun scribbling lots of lines for the pointy spines all over the hedgehog's back.

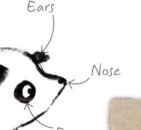

Hungry baby hedgehogs

Baby hedgehogs are called hoglets. How cute! They are born deaf and blind, and they have soft spines.

4 Add a few layers of shading to finish off your hedgehog.

Creepy-CRAWLIES

Ant

Ladybug

How do you feel about creepy-crawlies? Believe it or not, they're actually pretty important! Insects like buzzy bees and beautiful butterflies play a huge role in pollinating plants, and wiggly worms recycle what they eat, and their poop is great for the soil!

Let's give some bug drawings a try!

Ant

Ants live in groups called colonies. They are strong and can carry things that are heavier than they are!

1 Draw three circles—make sure the middle one is the smallest.

2 Add two curved lines for the antennae.

3 Draw in six lines for the legs and a circle with a dot for the eye. Add shading, too.

Ladybug

Most ladybugs have bright red wings with black spots. Did you know that if they're scared they play dead?

1 Draw a semicircle for the body, then add a small circle for the head.

2 Draw two lines for the antennae and a circle and dot for the eye.

3 Draw six **L** shapes for legs, scribbly spots, and shading.

Bumblebee

Sombre goldenring dragonfly

Common nawab butterfly

Bumblebee

Bumblebees are fuzzy with yellow-and-black stripes. Their delicate wings help them fly between flowers.

1 Draw an oval shape for the body.

2 Add two teardrop shapes for the wings.

3 Scribble in stripes, leaving two white dots for eyes. Add lines for legs and antennae, too.

Dragonfly

Dragonflies can be found near water. They have a long, slender body and two pairs of see-through wings.

1 Draw a cucumber shape for the body. Add two short lines for the antennae and an eye.

2 Then, add two long teardrops for the wings, and six lines for legs.

3 Add detail and shading to the wings and body.

Butterfly

Butterflies have large, colorful wings. They start life as a caterpillar, but later become a butterfly.

1 Draw a cucumber shape for the body and then add two lines for the antennae.

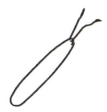

2 Next, add two teardrops, one big and one small for the wings.

3 Now, let's add a little eye and six lines for legs. Add some patterns and shapes to the wings, too.

That's staggering!

In addition to being superfast runners, deer are fantastic at jumping and can jump up to 10 ft (3 m) high—which is as high as a basketball hoop!

TIP
Try drawing a female deer without the antlers, too!

Dashing DEER

Deer are graceful animals that live in herds in forests, fields, and meadows. They have slender legs and a beautiful brown coat of fur. Deer are known for their antlers, but only the males, called stags, have these. Do you know how to draw a dashing deer?

1 Grab a pencil and draw a bean shape for the deer's body.

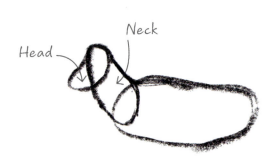

2 Next, draw in two more beans for the neck and head.

3 Now, draw two leaf-shaped ears and two dashes for the eye and nose. Don't forget the antlers—let's make them spiky!

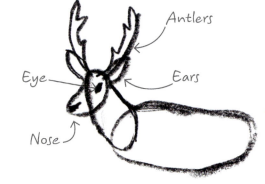

NOW TRY...

Every deer has a different pair of antlers. Why not have some fun trying to draw some?

Oh baby!

Did you know that baby deer are called fawns? They tend to have spotted fur to help them blend in with the tall grass.

Males use their antlers to protect themselves from predators.

4 Draw long sock shapes for the deer's legs.

Legs

5 Draw a little banana for the tail, and then it's time to add your shading. That looks great!

79

Brilliant BIRDS

There are more than 11,000 species of birds in the world and they are the only animals that have feathers. They all have wings, too, but not all of them can fly. They come in a range of colors and sizes, which is what makes them so much fun to draw!

Great horned owl

European robin

Owl

Also known as the tiger owl, this owl is found in the Americas and eats small animals, such as rabbits.

1 Draw a potato shape for the body, a triangle for a beak, two ovals for eyes, two leaves for ears, and a scribbly head marking.

2 Draw two circles with dots inside for the eyes, curved lines around the beak, and scribbles for wings.

3 Add vertical dashes for the feathered tummy, little lines for feet, then some shading.

Robin

European robins are small birds that have a distinctive orange tummy!

1 Draw a potato shape for the body, a triangle for the beak, and a dot for the eye.

2 Draw two diagonal lines for legs with four small lines for claws, and a scribbly wing, tail, and feathers.

3 Add some shading to make it more realistic.

Rock pigeon

Great spotted woodpecker

Chick

Pigeon

These gray birds have a pinkish tummy and a loud "coo" that is easy to recognize.

1 Draw an almond shape for the wing, a large curved line for the body, semicircle for the head, and a triangle for the beak.

2 Next, draw two **M** shapes for the claws, and a circle with a dot for the eye.

3 Add some feathers—zigzags on the head, wavy lines on the wing, and scallops on the tummy.

Woodpecker

Woodpeckers live in trees and hammer their beaks against trees to find food.

1 Sketch a circle for the head, a triangle for the beak, and a big semicircle for the body.

2 Then, draw a dot for the eye, a **Y** for the marking on the face, a scribbly wing and tail, and lines for the claws.

3 Finally, add pencil shading and paint for extra feathery details.

Chick

Chicks are baby chickens. They are adorable animals, and are yellow and really fluffy.

1 Draw a potato shape for the body, a triangle for the beak, and a dot for the eye.

2 Next, draw a scribbly wing, two lines for legs, and little lines for claws.

3 Add scallops for feathers and some shading, too.

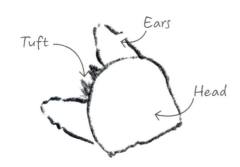

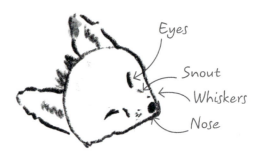

1 Start by drawing a rounded triangle shape for the head, two smaller triangle shapes for the ears, and a scribble for the tuft of fur.

2 Next, sketch two curved lines for the eyes, two dashes for the snout, a little black circle for the nose, and lines for whiskers.

3 Draw a big oval for the fox's back. Don't forget scribbles in the ears.

Out at night

Foxes are nocturnal, which means they come out at night, but they have excellent eyesight and can see in the dark!

TIP
Try coloring in your fox with watercolor paint.

Furry FOX

Foxes have beautiful brown and orange fur and a long, bushy tail. They mostly come out at night, and are known for being very smart and quick. Foxes live in homes called dens, and like to explore the woods and fields. Let's draw!

Can you hear that?

In addition to good eyesight, foxes also have incredible hearing. They can hear rodents digging underground from miles away!

A fox's fur is long and thick to keep it warm in winter.

4 Now, draw a hook shape for the fox's back leg and a curved line past the end of the nose to the fox's bottom to make a tail. Add a zigzag across the tail, too.

5 Add some scribbles for the fur.

6 Finally, finish your fox by adding some shading.

83

Brown BEAR

Bears are big, strong animals with thick, fuzzy fur and paws with claws. They are great at climbing trees, running, and swimming. Don't be fooled by how cuddly they look, these animals can be dangerous—so people should stay a safe distance away from them. Are you ready to draw a brown bear?

Life lessons

Mother bears are protective of their cubs. They teach their young how to survive and hunt in the wild.

1 First, let's draw a circle for the head.

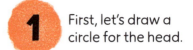

Head

2 Next, add in two semicircles for the ears. For the snout, draw an oval with a black circle near the end.

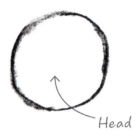

Ears

Snout

3 Add two dots for eyes and then two U shapes for the front legs.

Eyes

Front legs

Hibernation

Most brown bears spend the winter resting, or hibernating, in dens to avoid the cold weather. They stock up on food and then save their energy for the warmer months.

4 Add a big backward **C** shape for the bear's body.

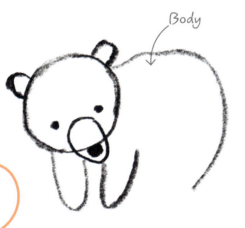

Body

5 Then, sketch two sock shapes for the back legs. Don't forget to add some little lines for the claws.

Claws

Back legs

6 Finally, add some scribbles for the fur to make it look fluffy!

TIP
Don't forget to add two black dots for the inside of the ears!

85

PAW PRINTS

You can find paw prints in mud, soil, and even snow. Some are small, like those of little mice, while others are large, like those of bears. When exploring animal tracks, you can learn a lot about the animal, such as its size, habitat, and potential hiding spots.

Cat

Cats have pads on the bottom of their paws to protect their feet.

 1  **2** Four ovals **3**

Jelly bean

Mouse

Mice have back paws similar to human feet, with five toes to help them run and jump.

1 Curve

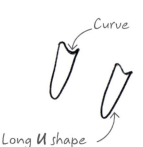

Long U shape

2 Circle **3** Five long sausages

Duck

Ducks have webbed feet that help them paddle through water.

1

V shape

2 Line down the middle

3 Two curves

86

Horse hoof

A horse is pretty heavy, and it has hard hooves to support its weight.

1 Circle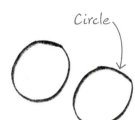

2 Erase a chunk and draw a V

3

Horseshoe

Some horses have shoes on the bottom of their hooves to help them walk on uneven ground.

1 U shape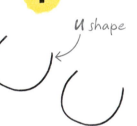

2 Smaller U / Two small lines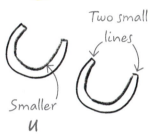

3

Bear

Bears have large padded paws with long, curved claws that help them dig up food and walk on different terrain.

1 Potato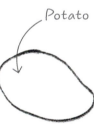

2 Five ovals

3

Rabbit

Rabbits have long, furry feet that keep their toes warm in various landscapes.

1 U shape

2 Spikes

3

Fun FORMULAS

You've learned to draw a lot of animals in this book. Here is a quick reminder of what shapes and lines to use to draw each critter!

Cat

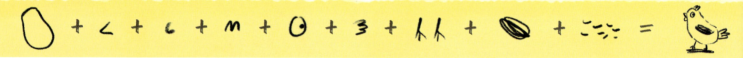

Chicken

Bunny

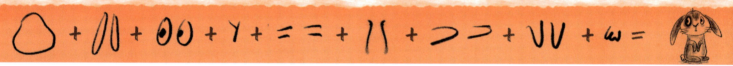

Guinea pig

Hamster

Mouse

Duckling

Dog

Lemur

Giraffe

Sloth

Elephant

Cheetah

Tiger

Wallaby
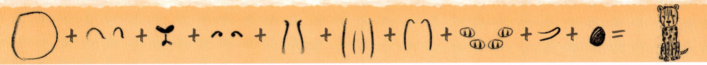

Monkey

Turtle
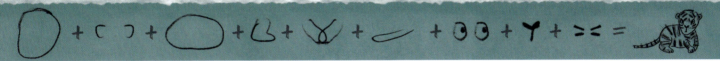

Octopus
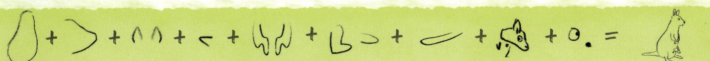

Penguin

Jellyfish

Starfish

Dolphin

Shark

Goat

Donkey

Horse

Cow

Sheep

Pig
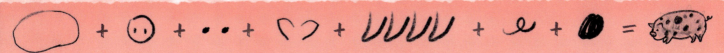

Llama
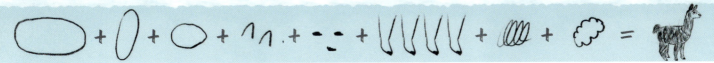

Alpaca

Frog
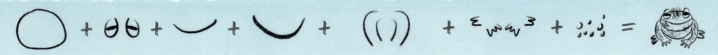

Beaver
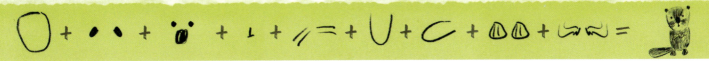

Squirrel

Hedgehog

Deer

Fox

Bear

Time for COLOR!

Now that you have drawn all of your favorite animals, it is time to add some color! Grab some of your color materials and let's get creative...

Butterflies are bright, so be bold with the colors that you choose!

BUTTERFLY

SQUIRREL

LADYBUG

GIRAFFE

TIP
Use different tones of the same color to add depth and shadows.

TIGER

INDEX

A
acrylic paints 15
air drawing 7
alpacas 69, 91
angelfish 53
antlers 79
ants 76

B
baby animals
 bear cubs 84
 chicks 81
 elephants 37
 fawns 79
 Henrietta the duckling 26–27, 88
 hoglets 75
 horses 61
 lambs 65
 monkeys 44
 penguins 50
 pointer puppies 29
 wallabies 43
ballpoint pens 12
bats 9
bears 84–85, 91
 paw prints 87
beavers 72–73, 91
bees 93
birds 80–81, 93
 Cilla the chicken 20–21
 feathers 21, 27
 footprints 86
 Henrietta the duckling 26–27, 88
 penguins 50–51
 shapes of 9
blindfolded drawing 6
bumblebees 77
bunnies 88
 Buzz the bunny 22
butterflies 77, 92

C
camouflage 35
Caramel the guinea pig 23, 88
cats 88
 paw prints 86
 Jessie the cat 19
cecropia leaves 34
chalk 14
chameleon 17, 40–41
cheetahs 38, 89
chicken 88
 chicks 81
 Cilla the chicken 20–21
chicks
 chicken 81
 penguin 50
Cilla the chicken 20–21
clown fish 53
color
 adding color 92–93
 color blindness 16
 the color wheel 16
 colored materials 14–15
 contrasting colors 17
 different colors 16
 mixing colors 17
 primary colors 16
 secondary colors 16
 tones 92
contrasting colors 17
cows 62–63, 90
crayons 15
creepy-crawlies 76–77
crocodiles 40–41
cubs 84

D
deer 78–79, 91
dogs 88
 pointer puppies 29
 poodles 29
 types of 28
 Winter the dog 28–29
dolphins 56, 90

donkeys 60, 90
dragonflies 77
ducks and ducklings 9, 26, 88
 feathers 27
 footprints 86
 Henrietta the duckling 26–27
 runner ducks 27

E
elephants 36–37, 89

F
farm animals 58–69
feathers 21, 27
feet
 ducks' 27
 frogs' 71
 goats' 59
felt-tip pens 15
fine-tipped markers 12
fish 52–53
flamingos 9
footprints 86–87
forest friends 70–87
formulas 88–91
fountain pens 13
foxes 82–83, 91, 93
frogs 71, 91
fur
 foxes' 83
 giraffes' 33
 hamsters' 24
 sloths' 35

G
geckos 40–41
giraffes 32–33, 89, 92
goats 59, 90
guinea pig, Caramel the 23, 88

94

H
hamster, Hugo the 24, 88
hedgehogs 75, 91
Henrietta the duckling 26–27
Highland cow 63
hippopotamus 9
horses 61, 90
　hoofprints 87
　horseshoes 87
Hugo the hamster 24, 88

I, J, K
insects 76–77
jellyfish 54, 90
Jessie the cat 19
koalas 9

L
ladybugs 76, 92
lambs 65
leaves, cecropia 34
lemurs 31, 89
letters 8
lines 10
　thick vs. thin lines 33
llamas 68, 91

M
mark making 10–11
markers 12
materials, colored 14–15
mice 88
　Millie the mouse 25
　paw prints 86
microcanthus 52
Millie the mouse 25
monkeys 44–45, 89

O
octopus 48–49, 89, 93
opposite hand drawing 6
otters 9
owls 80, 93

P
paints 15
pandas 9
panther grouper 52
pastels 14
paw prints 86–87
pencils 12, 15
penguins 50–51, 90
　rockhopper penguins 51
pens 12–13, 15
pets 18–29
pigeons 81
pigs 66–67, 91
Pippa's pets 18–29
plumage 21, 27
pointer puppies 29
poodles 29
primary colors 16
puffer fish 53

R
rabbits 88
　Buzz the bunny 22
　paw prints 87
reptiles 40–41
robins 80
rockhopper penguins 51
runner ducks 27

S
sea creatures 46–57
secondary colors 16
shading 11, 21
shapes
　basic shapes 8
　spotting shapes 8–9
sharks 57, 90
sheep 64–65, 90
sloths 34–35, 89
snakes 40–41
spotted fish 52
squirrels 74, 91, 92
starfish 55, 90
stars, drawing 55
striped fish 52
swirly fish 53

T
tails 25
　lemurs' 31
　pigs' 67
　squirrels' 74
taking a line for a walk 7
tigers 9, 39, 89, 92
tones 92
toucans 9
turtles 47, 89

U, W
under the sea 46–57
wallabies 42–43, 89, 93
warm-up exercises 6–7
watercolor paints 15, 93
wax crayons 15
whales 9
wild animals 30–45
Winter the dog 28–29
woodpeckers 81

95

About PIPPA

Pippa Pixley lives in the heart of the Peak District National Park, nestled among the hills of the dragon's back. She lives with her husband, three playful children, a lovable dog, a fluffy herd of Angora rabbits, and a growing family of amazing animals. Pippa loves spending time outside in nature, where she draws, scribbles, and sketches all the wonderful critters she discovers and observes. It's like having a real-life adventure every day!

Acknowledgments

DK would like to thank the following people for their assistance in the preparation of this book: Sakshi Saluja for picture research, Laura Gilbert for proofreading, and Vanessa Bird for compiling the index.

The publisher would like to thank the following for their kind permission to reproduce their photographs:

(Key: a-above; b-below/bottom; c-centre; f-far; l-left; r-right; t-top)

1 Fotolia: picsfive (c). **6 123RF.com:** Oleksiy (cl). **6-7 Dreamstime.com:** Les Cunliffe (c). **9 Dreamstime.com:** Volodymyr Byrdyak (tr); Simone Gatterwe / Smgirly (ca); Sombra12 (cl); Isselee (cb, crb); Lianquan Yu (br). **Fotolia:** picsfive (tl). **11 123RF.com:** Oleksiy (cla). **Dorling Kindersley:** Rotring UK Ltd (tr). **Dreamstime.com:** Joingate. **Fotolia:** picsfive (tc). **12-13 Dreamstime.com:** David M. Schrader. **12 123RF.com:** Oleksiy (clb). **Dorling Kindersley:** Rotring UK Ltd (clb/Red pencil). **13 Dreamstime.com:** Vapsik662 (bl). **Fotolia:** picsfive (clb). **14 Dreamstime.com:** Songdech Kothmongkol (bl); Rudchenko (clb). **14–15 Dreamstime.com:** David M. Schrader. **15 Dreamstime.com:** Lightpainter (cra); Becky Starsmore (tr). **16 Dreamstime.com:** Megan Lorenz (bl). **17 Dreamstime.com:** Dmitry Petlin (crb). **20 Dreamstime.com:** Constantin Mihai (bl). **21 Alamy Stock Photo:** Krys Bailey (tc). **Dreamstime.com:** andreykuzmin (tr); Sikth (ca). **22 Shutterstock.com:** Sven Boettcher (cl). **23 Alamy Stock Photo:** Juniors Bildarchiv / F300 (ca). **24 123RF.com:** picsfive (br). **Alamy Stock Photo:** Design Pics / Radius Images (clb). **Dreamstime.com:** Oksana Ermak (bl). **25 Alamy Stock Photo:** blickwinkel / H. Duty (cra). **26 Dreamstime.com:** Gale Verhague (cl). **Getty Images:** Don Farrall / Photodisc (bl). **27 Dreamstime.com:** Susan Quinland Stringer (tl). **Fotolia:** picsfive (tc). **28 123RF.com:** Eric Isselee (clb). **29 Dreamstime.com:** Robyn Mackenzie / Robynmac (r); Shevs (tl). **Fotolia:** picsfive (ca). **31 Dreamstime.com:** Lunamarina (clb). **32 123RF.com:** Magdalena Paluchowska (tl). **Dreamstime.com:** Dragoneye (bl). **33 Dreamstime.com:** Jenya Pavlovski (tr). **Fotolia:** picsfive (tc). **34 Alamy Stock Photo:** Suzi Eszterhas / Minden Pictures (clb). **Dreamstime.com:** Harry Collins (cl). **35 Dreamstime.com:** Kungverylucky (clb, tr); Spolcycstudio (ca). **36 Dreamstime.com:** Dmytro Gilitukha (cl); Vladvitek (crb). **37 Dreamstime.com:** Ildi900 (cra); Leonmaraisphoto (tl). **38 Dreamstime.com:** Isselee (tc); Stu Porter (c). **39 Dreamstime.com:** Appfind (cra); Nilanjan Bhattacharya (tr). **40 Dreamstime.com:** Dmitry Petlin (bl). **42 Dreamstime.com:** Dirkr (bl); Isselee (cr). **43 Dreamstime.com:** Nawors (c); Robyn Mackenzie / Robynmac (br). **44 Dreamstime.com:** Dolphfyn (cb); Eric Gevaert (clb). **45 Dreamstime.com:** Ittipon (tr). **Fotolia:** picsfive (tc). **47 Dreamstime.com:** Viacheslav Dubrovin (tl). **48 Dreamstime.com:** Demin Pan (cl); Jeffrey Walthall (bl); Surabhi25 (br). **49 Dreamstime.com:** Henner Damke (tr). **50 Dreamstime.com:** Inaras (cb). **Getty Images:** Fuse (tl). **51 Dreamstime.com:** Lizgiv (bl); Michael Rolands / Mrolands (tl). **Fotolia:** picsfive (tr). **52 Dreamstime.com:** Diego Grandi (tc); Mirecca (tr). **53 Dreamstime.com:** Cynoclub (tr); Eric Isselâe / Isselee (tl); Johannesk (tc). **54 123RF.com:** Pavlo Vakhrushev / vapi (tl). **Dreamstime.com:** Gary Parker (cl). **55 Alamy Stock Photo:** Nigel Sawyer (cra). **56 Dreamstime.com:** Willyambradberry (cl). **57 Dorling Kindersley:** Terry Goss (tr). **Dreamstime.com:** Bcpix (cr). **59 Dorling Kindersley:** South of England Rare Breeds Centre, Ashford, Kent (tl). **Getty Images / iStock:** technotr (cr). **60 Dreamstime.com:** Elena Titarenco (cl). **61 123RF.com:** Olga Itina (cr). **62 Dreamstime.com:** Supertrooper (br). **63 Dreamstime.com:** Joaquin Corbalan (tl). **Fotolia:** picsfive (tr). **64 Dreamstime.com:** Sergii Figurnyi (cla); Ksena2009 (br). **65 123RF.com:** Piyawat Nandeenopparit (bl). **Fotolia:** picsfive (tl). **66 Alamy Stock Photo:** Wayne Hutchinson (tl). **Dreamstime.com:** Susansanger (clb). **67 Dreamstime.com:** Elenavolf (crb); Voratham Yuangngoen (tr). **Fotolia:** picsfive (tl). **68 123RF.com:** Eric Isselee / isselee (tl). **Alamy Stock Photo:** Pep Roig (tr). **69 Dreamstime.com:** Robyn Mackenzie (cr); Yurasova (tl). **71 123RF.com:** Eric Isselee (cla). **Dreamstime.com:** Hotshotsworldwide (cr). **72 Dreamstime.com:** Charles Dyer (clb); Jnjhuz (tr). **73 Dreamstime.com:** Aline Bedard (tr); Crystalseye (tl). **Fotolia:** picsfive (tl). **74 Dorling Kindersley:** British Wildlife Centre, Surrey, UK (cr). **75 Dreamstime.com:** Freelancer74 (cr); Eric Isselee (tr). **76 123RF.com:** Alexandr Pakhnyushchyy / alekss (tc); Oleksiy (clb). **77 Dreamstime.com:** Isselee (tc); Sutisa Kangvansap / Mathisa (tr). **78 Dreamstime.com:** Slowmotiongli (tl). **Fotolia:** anankkml (clb). **79 Dorling Kindersley:** British Wildlife Centre, Surrey, UK (c). **Dreamstime.com:** Paul Farnfield (tr). **Fotolia:** picsfive (tl). **80 Dreamstime.com:** Vasyl Helevachuk (tr); Stephen Mcsweeny (tc). **81 Dorling Kindersley:** Neil Fletcher (tl). **Dreamstime.com:** Eng101 (tc). **82 Dreamstime.com:** Justinhoffmanoutdoors (br); Dalia Kvedaraite (cl). **83 Dreamstime.com:** Jurga Basinskaite (cra); Mbridger68 (tc). **84 Dreamstime.com:** Sergey Uryadnikov (clb). **85 Alamy Stock Photo:** Juniors Bildarchiv / R304 (tr). **86 123RF.com:** ksena32 (cla); schan (cl). **Dreamstime.com:** Isselee (bl). **87 Dreamstime.com:** Anjajuli (tr); Miketanct (cr); Kyolshin (br)

Cover images: Front: **123RF.com:** Oleksiy bl; **Dreamstime.com:** Joingate c